STRAWBERRIES
UNDER SKIN

STRAWBERRIES UNDER SKIN

POEMS

NIHARIKA SHAH

NEW DEGREE PRESS

COPYRIGHT © 2021 NIHARIKA SHAH

STRAWBERRIES UNDER SKIN

ISBN   978-1-63730-371-9   *Paperback*

         978-1-63730-372-6   *Kindle Ebook*

         978-1-63730-373-3   *Ebook*

For Niki Di
my sister, my strongest pillar

CONTENTS

———

To Me. 49

AUTHOR'S NOTE

———

Dear Reader,

That you are holding this book in your hands right now, engaging in this physical experience with its pages, picking up and tracing the outline of every word that represents a slice of who I am, feels surreal.

Strawberries Under Skin is a vessel, a trove of every town I've moved to, every house I've called home, every body I've tried to live in and person I've wanted to live for. This book makes promises. And breaks them. It invites you into a dream-like love and then makes you watch as it slowly dissipates. It is confessional and proud. It is brave because it strives to break the 'standard.' It is honest. It is me.

I started working on *Strawberries Under Skin* at a time I didn't know I'd ever write a book. I was just another girl who'd stumbled upon love, allowed herself to be broken apart by it, and eventually discovered healing from it. Wide-eyed and trusting, I thought the only way to get over a seventeen-year-old boy was to turn him into poetry. And since nobody ever questioned my methods, it soon became a habit to turn every dying thing into art.

Strawberries speaks of nothing but the truth, and part of being honest is recognizing the root. I'm aware I could come across as the sad girl who writes about her broken heart. But there are two things my elders have taught me that I think about every day: *be thankful for the things you are blessed with* and *remember that pain comes in equal shares for everybody.* I should not be ashamed to write about my pain, especially if I am celebrating the part where I got through it. I used to let a lot of people and external factors dictate the cause and subject of my writing until one day I decided I was not going to allow anybody to limit me like that. I remember sitting in my dorm room, mid-second year, with my eyes focused on the computer screen, and fingers plopped on the keyboard. Carefully, I entered the words *Economics* ... and *English* as my intended double major, knowing fully well this decision would not be welcomed with open arms in my community. All these years, I had been walking with this incredibly heavy weight that was constraining several choices I didn't know I was allowed to even make, but I was no longer going to let anybody else tell me what dreams I should dream, and which is the more acceptable way to earn a living and the respect of my community.

Today, I let go of that weight.

I release myself.

And this book is my gift, to you.

It is a tribute to love. It is a letter to the people who have helped me write it. It is testimony to change. It is a haven for those who have not yet found comfort in their own skin, body, and choices. It is a home for those gone astray. I started to compile this book with the hope that the love I write so exquisitely about unifies all my readers and reminds them that they're not alone in this journey of putting themselves back together and liberating their spirits to be unapologetically themselves.

As you move through the three chapters, the poems will move with you, and you will experience a shift in style and intent. These transitions are purposeful, reminding you of how things can change for the better. I have chosen to write about very different relationships with the self, the body, and to those who have broken and built it, but in all my writing experience, I have never turned to love and found that it is not there. Love has and always will be my starting point for everything.

I hope that I can offer you a little bit of peace, amidst all of this chaos that is still whirling in and around us. I would like for you to get to know me, and I cannot imagine a better introduction than by inviting you to read me. I hope that my words encourage you to explore all the different corners of your heart and celebrate its every fold and tear.

I didn't grow up with icons to look up to—distinctive personalities that had braved familial and societal stigmas around the desire to follow their dreams of becoming a notable author, poet, or artist. I had to fight the norm every step of the way. I had to fight convention. I had to take the decision at the tender age of nineteen to become that someone I never had: a ray of inspiration for the next generation of dreamers, so that they wouldn't have to fight as hard to want their dreams to be recognized. This is the first step of my journey. And I have so much more to go. So many more people to reach. Here, you are literally under my skin.

Thanks for stopping by.

Love,
Niharika

TO YOU.

—

"Yes, there is a place where someone loves you both before and after they learn what you are."

– NEIL HILBORN, "LAKE," THE FUTURE

paper boat hats

the lights went out or maybe you turned
them down, i couldn't tell, but the dark
appeared less violent, less damned—

an appetizer for two hungry vagrants
with paper boats for hats.

time lost its tempo and my inhibitions,
tucked neatly inside the heart of a blue satin thong.
fell to my knees, hands locked securely
before my chest

folded in prayer, i looked to you and asked,
why, why did god send me to you?

you pulled my gaze toward your gaping
mouth so i could watch you bubble answers
out in breaths.

a sailor's type of sickness—
a stomach-turning thirst for forgiving
your lips for peeling off of my lips
one stretch of skin at a time

and you sighed,
with the shadow of a smile
and ghosts in your eyes,

to save me.

space

you're
the sun
you radiate the truth and warmth i wish to don

you're
the moon
you absorb all light and effuse it out of your craters until it
is morn

you're
the universe
that engulfs my body whole, when two lifeless orbs collide,
where good is born

melodies

you plucked
the broken strings of my guitar
and created melodies unheard of

there's a name for such a kind
of brokenness

symphony
  catastrophe
    love

magnets

i was cotton yesterday
today,
steel

see, i thought you were just my magnet

you
are
gravity.

This Night

I know it seems
Our hands may slip,
But hold on tight.

If you're afraid
To brush my lips
With yours, so light

Then do it quicker
Than before,
We've just this night.

pink strawberry milk

he says he can feel his heart getting buried under pink
strawberry milk

he's never had strawberry milk before
but he knows i like sucking on the fruit like a child does,
a popsicle

he says he's falling
and cannot tell if this falling feels like a plummet from a
cliff into a river
no life vests

or an earthward drop down a hole in the ground swirling
like a gush of past
forgotten

it's deafening, by the station,
i must cover my ears with mittens to even
think of him
i like to think of him
in volume

but the trains and all their whistles
morning walks to Depot fizzle
into two-thirds an *i love y*—

bell towers chime the chorus six or seven times

and i quietly hum along

we don't want to say goodbye so we choose
to not say anything
but the trains go home with people going home to other people
like it's normal

there's something so remarkable
about getting to your destination, your final stop,
your person

i remember winding and unwinding into him

reminds me of the night we danced
to vodka and a nascent love
he spoke his first *i love you* and it was
full

and he drank his whiskey straight said he preferred
to light my lips on fire said maybe
then just maybe
he could smoke them

the high lasts longer
he said, made him feel like he could age
in reverse

he is dripping
soul thick, over layers
and layers of vanilla yogurt lies, he's been running

for so long he's forgotten what's been running after him,
what is left
to even run towards

so i stop him

put my hand over his chest to remind him he's allowed
to breathe

i pour
100 mL of me in

he feels heavier

and he says he wants to never feel light again.

stars

I want to tell the stars about you

but they're already burning

and dying

is fated for everything born

of matter

and had there been more suns

to pray to

I would tell them of your

love

and how it burned

all we touched

to cinder.

amaranthine

it's a strange kind of world
we thirst for people
and settle for tonic
vodka tonic

you just left
and a strange sense of déjà vu
lurks at the corner of my lip

strokes the rim of my tarnished tumbler
soft
and tender
a kind of larceny tried only at the hip

what passion—what lust—
with what godly devotion
do i shiver

i bleed
i blush afraid that the color in my cheek
drains all the way down to my panties
this must be funny

but you smile, say,
you now have all the red you'll ever need
to paint fires burning down the forests

my tumbler's almost empty
but i will not fill it up, i will not clean

because i can still smell you
near the foot of dirty things

amaranthine, you call me,
when i shed some of my underskin
and you ask for second servings

you kiss mountain tops the same way you kneel
before its footing
with sinful care

like they destroy you
and you devour them
(heedless to which comes first)

you press your hands steady over mine
let the wind take its course
allow the calamity to

blow us up

i hate victims
yet you aim for my thighs, your tongue
pulls the trigger

i love being your casualty.

should you kiss me

i have a thing for being slammed against walls
something about being held together
end to end

only poetry

i left the water running
over both my hands too long
now my finger's skin is pruney
are you poetry?
can you tell
why these hands soaked in water
look like deserts?
this mouth feels silenced
like a lamb inside an abattoir
are you poetry?
can you tell me why i fell
for eyes that would not
even look at me?
are you poetry?
does that mean that i can
touch you, that you will be a
standing joke for all the
sciences, that you'll always be my
sin, never
salvation?

Write for me

Will you write for me?
If I say your words can save me
If I say your art can heal me
Will you try?

Will you draw for me?
If I pull my arm apart for you
Trim my fingernails, hand a brush to you
Should I try?

Where's your masterpiece?
Bare canvas, left my chest open for you
Plunged a needle inside, drained my blood for you
Is it dry?

Where's the life in me?
Did you paint a couple hearts in red
Or was it pink? Perhaps the colors bled

Did I die?

All love hurts

Mama's love hurts my nose
when she calls me a waste of time and breath,
it hurts to swallow air.

Papa's love hurts in the stomach
like it can't contain the skin that sheds
when he catches me talking to a boy till late
who will never learn   to   stay.

Tuff's love hurts all over my palms
the ends of my fingers that reminisce in
the shadows of his velvet soft ears.
They still search for him in empty closet shelves,
on cold bathroom floors and the kennel that stays
open all day—we don't latch the gate anymore.

And then there is *your* love
that lights my chest on fire
like I'm burning, screaming,
and you're holding ice in your hands
but you slip it in cola and douse it—

perhaps I'm standing at a blind spot
you can't tell that I'm being stifled—
I am charring, fully blackened at the edges,
as you moan about the smoke,
the way it makes you sweat.

I am drowning
and I can't call for help because I know if you try and save me,
I will never swim again.

castles are also called ruins

I'm sorry I am so soft

I thought I wanted you to touch me

I didn't know I'd dis
                    in
                       tegrate

the reason

are you the reason why the days are bright
and poets make love on bare walls at night

love spits out words they paint in red
on thighs and foreheads; they put love to bed

"what was it like to love me?"

loving you
is draining
like a cloth wringing
blood
and water from the
bucket mama said
not to touch
so much blood
is draining
every last shred of
will
i have left inside
to keep on
loving you
hurts
to keep on
loving you
pushes boulders
down my
chest like
loving you
means walking
with shoulders
that don't want
to carry me
any more.

If tomorrow starts without me

If tomorrow starts without me
I hope it rains buttercups
wherever you are.
I hope you stick your tongue out
and it tastes like burnt breadcrumbs.
I hope you find exactly what you've been
looking for
and realize that you've wasted so
many birthday
wishes, wishing
for the wrong things.
You could love me for my blatant
mediocrity
but you don't.
You want buttercups and butterscotch
and I'm sorry I could never
be anything
more
than a bunch of red roses
and vanilla.

Paper Films

Nightfall brings
exhaustion, chills, nightingales sing
sad lullabies unheard of.
They wince
as I wince when a lightning bolt strikes my chest.

Paper films
fade to dust, speak of tales so whim—
sical, mock the misery
we were
but the worthless, frail little pigeon you called

me stung. Hard.
I'm spent from apologizing
drained from weeks of ruing; I
fucked up.
But the sun continues to shine every morn

and I don't.
I can scream that I'm repentant
but if you cannot see me
quiver
against the wind for your embrace—let me go.

confession

writing
about you
is like a cold wet tissue
over sunburnt skin

temporary,

but *god*
does it feel good.

Longing in warehouses

It is a different kind of aching, to want you.
  Like a drainpipe but for my stomach, the way it pulls
  and plunges out your toxins.

To know, I cannot have you.
  Like trucks that leave their skid marks on my chest, I
  cannot tell if they are lost   or if they like to run
  in circles.

Or that, I shouldn't.
  Says your pendant resting softly on my neck—presses
  kisses and the air inside my lungs happens to dissipate.

All day, I hear them crying
  My chest, my gut, my lungs, they cry *I need you*
  It's a shame that you can't hear it

You can't hear any of it.

truth or dare

    comes
truth ~~hurts~~ easy / when it's pouring out / your lips / softening
the wounds of gunshot bliss / skin on skin in cotton / dipped /
in antiseptic whiskeys and gins / a love affair so toxic / free
to kill / us both / and like most truths /
we let it /

5:07 pm

i keep chasing the sun
it keeps running away from me

Don't Stop Loving Me

Don't.

Don't stop.

Don't stop loving.

Don't stop loving me.

I crumble
  like icing
    on a cake tower
      hot from the oven
        you have to learn   to be gentle

Don't stop loving.

It makes you who you are

Saltwater taffy peppermint

Spicy & tangerine

You don't come without

Your kinks.

Don't stop.

It's harder to start

Again so let's not

Stop at rest stops

& gas stations.

Commercials annoy

The both of us so

> When I ask you
> to give us
> a break—

> Don't.

Say no.
To pauses
& talking over each other
& mood swings louder
Than the one on our porch.

Say no
& let it roll over
into a snowball
rolling & rolling &
hear it echo
our prayers—

Don't stop loving me.

Don't stop loving.

Don't stop.

Don't.

Ode to Your Body

O sweet eyes;
Big, beautiful, dark chocolate eyes that harbor sniffles, sins
that smell of sights that shriveled— dwindled into thoughts
forgotten. You like to push soft sentiment to the back and
swaddle it with bandage for no one to ever see. But I saw you,
on a summer day in June and I asked you to come out and
get some air. I may not be around anymore to hold your lids
that quiver in acquiescence, but leave the weapons be, and
let your deluge outpour all the monsoons past.

O rebel hair;
Ruffled, curly, black as ink, follows no instruction, spray of
ants running riot running home. You shield him from the
pouring rain and guard him from the sun. You smear an
ugly tan across his brow that he hates he can't discolor. I
am sorry he fails to see the good in the world; it hasn't seen
enough of it in him. I am sorry I spared only seconds today
to run through your morning-fresh thicket; you never know
your last good day is your last good day till it is. Or I would
have buried my fingers deep into your skull, felt the roots
sprouting under my thumb and fore fingers, watched them
slip, unfurl like a pretty black ribbon, and depart.

O gentle hands;
You wide-eyed, impatient, and certain, decisive hands. You
traced the outline of my face, ran a quiet distance between

my set of ears, asymmetrical and coy. And excavated mine-shafts in the folds of my inner thighs, you looked for rubies and forgotten first-lights. It was you I said goodbye to at-last, when you brushed against my wrist like two old friends too shy to speak their minds, too far gone to whisper *please, stay.*

O gallant spine;
Tall, vertical, dauntless spine, that part of him that holds his neck up straight, his eyes in line with where his vision intends to take him. It is you he thinks of most, and only you he will ever expect from. You wiped his blood clean and warmed his toes a toasty pink. You didn't break when he was whiplashed, when he hunched, when he lost his first love. You were carrying books in backpacks and stones in leather knapsacks and every person's last farewell to him. Be loyal. Midst those who try to put him down, you keep him brave and burning.

O funny elbow;
Odd, twisted, rough ol' elbow kept secret from the rest of your family. Say, do you feel small and pointless? Your shade's a darker brown, you're not exactly round, but if it weren't for you, his face and fingers would settle last as strained and distant lovers. He eats because you fold. He writes because you bend. You may not be the prettiest but you're a tough one to replace. The black sheep of the family—still family.

O weary legs;
Quick, venous, slender legs that carry the weight of every-
thing that makes him. You're remembered—your praises line
the walls of auditoriums. With you, he sailed through to the
finish lines and the podiums, and the crowds that cheered
his name, cheered for you. He learnt to cross the bridge with
half a heart and one open sleeve. With you, he came to me.

Protect him, through all ends and all beginnings.
Promise, that he'll never know our secret. That you
will not ever fail him, and he will not question why.
And when the whole world gives up on him the way he
gave up on me, swear that you will steer him forth.

When Bon Iver Sang That Song
About Defending His Homeland

I used to run toward you like a child away
   from the dark   I would run like I didn't know there was
anywhere else I could go

like the parts of me and the parts of you we somehow
learnt to tolerate
   I superglued together and called it home

I forgot   people capable of building windows
   are also capable of breaking doors down

I don't remember the last time I used these hands
   to pray
      for myself

the last time I slept   without wanting to fill the silence
   between the gaps in my breaths
      the last time I gave somebody the power
      to be known   as my homeland

there is nomoreland to cover love
   no calvary   no cross to carry through.

TO ME.

―――

"I believe a strong woman may be stronger than a man, particularly if she happens to have love in her heart. I guess a loving woman is indestructible."

– JOHN STEINBECK

how dare you sing sad songs about pain

god, neha you're so weak
you're so obsessed with pain
you cuddle it to sleep & pretend its
long barbed wires make for headrests

jesus christ could you for once
ask your body to not quit
being a body could you ask
for it not to shut down

look at you neha look
at you fumbling for twenty
twenty vision pick up the
damned duster & clean

the fucking concrete if
you love the floor so much
why don't you just marry it
maybe then you won't cheat

on it the ceiling's too far up
your league to notice but you
think you've got a conscience
& prostration is repentance

it's like you like to give yourself
fevers so he said he wished you left
because adulterers abandon it must
pinch when he calls you an adulterer

don't get confused honey the room
has air your body just rejects it
your body is a checkerboard
your mind plays all the white marbles

and there's this thing about escaping
the slammer when you haven't served
your time—you will always be
reminded of your treachery

no he's not likely to forgive you
but he'll love you and you won't
know better than to believe him
which means

you can sing your sad songs
in the evenings

you don't have to feign courage
in midwinter

you don't have to love yourself
today

In

After Thomas Sayers Ellis

In tins of
pink, forbidden
pringles
your fingers sin
   temptation sings

In spite of striving
not to sink further
into him—
your oars
   give in

In every pin
you prick, your
finger twinges, brings
you guilt
   and gin

In still waters
instill your lips
rinse,
the shame off
   your skin

In inhaling
sinsemilla, you spin,
you yearn for
   oxygen.

my therapist says

my therapist says don't put yourself in glass houses expecting to stop people from throwing stones /

as if that would stop them from throwing stones /

as if that would stop me from throwing myself / into houses made of thorns / floored with spilled milk / houses burning / roofs down / all the potted plants / are dying /

she says you're so afraid to let somebody in with tools / doesn't know that i'm afraid of blood and splinters / that clowns don't excite me / I am not a funny person / I don't like when I'm made fun of / but I laugh

so easy / leave them wondering if their jokes are that amusing / I am just a people-pleaser / nobody wants to please /

it's easy being pretty / doesn't pretty make life convenient / pretty girls / pretty flowers in pretty glass vases / pretty please / can I stay a little longer / these pages aren't finished / I'm afraid / when I run out of glass I will cut into my skin and build homes for runners that will never learn to stay /

For S

you didn't know but you were feeding me art

दुःख से बचने के लिए
दुःख को इतना पास रखना चाहती हो

  संभल के
  पैरों तले दब न जाना |

to save yourself from pain
you like to hold on to it, keep it close,

  careful
  lest it crush you neath its feet.

THINGS I NO LONGER WISH TO UNDERSTAND

- Why pages fold at the corners when I try to hold them down with my pen cap. Why they won't sit still.

- "I didn't mean it."

- A world where marriage is a contract, begging to find loopholes.

- *"I was high."*

- Loopholes.

- Why I am asked to stop fidgeting like my shaking leg bothers the half-bitten nails in your pocket, your dis/order/ that helps mask your dis/order/

- Self-deprecating humor

- "This is who I am."

- You must be so bored. This isn't even a poem.

- Why you won't give me what I want

- Why you won't be.

   A handkerchief to soak my complexities, a space for me to dissolve.

- Love and all its numbers. Just how many times does it expect to fall into my lap and crawl out of it?

- I am running out of days, they are running out of me.

her bathroom is her sanctum, and she cries there

7:39 pm and she stood there, in her bathroom, staring down a broken reflection, dabbing wet cheeks with a towel and a blender, both pink and soaking—*they must have slipped into the sink*, she thought, *somebody left the tap running.*

with a nose as red as the stone that rests on the forefront of her open chest, she wished for the blinking of a call. a voice that would settle its illusory arms round her shoulder and calm her cultured quivering, whisper, *wipe your tears dry, my love, the sun hasn't set on us yet.*

she clenched her eyes into a tight fist, so she might pray her demons away. she didn't want a world where she couldn't see the salsa dripping down his cherry lower lip, or feel his kisses break for breath and fingers lock into vortices inside her belly. his voicemails would quickly get lost in the clutter and his pink pepper perfume would fade but if she waited, perhaps, only half a minute longer, he could return. to the boy she once knew. she truly believed that if she stayed, he'd stay.

but it wasn't 11:11 and all she heard was gut-wrenching silence. he appeared, an apparition, holding his bloody, beating heart outside of his body and even then, the voices she imagined would propel her towards him, somehow, hushed. in her shameful attempt to prolong her stay in the pretty little cubicle by the doorway, she flushed down her prayers with pee. she almost dialed the number and then her phone fell. she forgot the *five second rule* he'd taught her for all things that fall to the ground—*you leave them be*, he said, *you never pick them up.* and his right hand on her left cheek stormed in at five, his impenitence at four, a tremor and a low sounding murmur at three, his ringtone at two, and at one, she put her phone down.

7:47 pm, and she debated standing underneath the shower, unsure if her shoulders would welcome a touch that searing again. she cried there. she broke into seven ugly pieces and cut their corners out. then she pulled out a tape and glue gun and sat to piece them all together again. with a puffed-up face, pink and torpid, and a chopstick holding her hair up-knot, she walked out. taller than the girl she was when she'd entered.

she was all she had in the world now. she belonged only to herself.

self-respect is a phoney bitch

I chose myself.
I rose above the swordfight you brought guns to
I learnt to walk away
from all that
violence
now I'm free
I am oh   so   free

   and alone.

Breeding ground

You know that worms live inside your stomach.

Mosquitos breed in dark quarters
of your cooler.

My dog has fleas that mate in the climate
of underarms.

(I wish I could be more erotic about this;
I wish I could be more erotic about it all)

You know what they call a group of newborn
flea babies?

An infestation.

Feed me the soles of your shoes for breakfast
(the ones you keep complaining I haven't walked in)

and I'll come back for second servings.

My flesh is like a nursery kept moist
and warm by arm strokes born in tundra.

It appears I cannot thrive as a poet unless
my heart is perpetually breaking.

Prose

It's a Thursday

when he turns to me, as I lay out the paper plates for take-out, and opens his mouth as if to speak, but doesn't. With one shrug, a deep breath sucked in from his stomach, and an uncertain retreat of his pale, sweaty hands, he blurts a bubble of words that float across in soundwaves
slow, until they finally strike the skin folding into the insides of my ear and—

thump

'I don't think I can be with you anymore,'

The soundwaves disappear, in fact, there is no sound at all.

thump

waves continue

'I have been meaning to get this out for weeks now but couldn't build up the courage because… well, because I was scared. I *am* scared, of what this will do to you, to us, but I cannot hold it in any longer.
It's weighing me down.'

PAUSE

'I'm sorry.'

thump

P A U S E

The human brain takes approximately 0.3 seconds to process a signal.
This Thursday
it takes longer.

Question emerges from my lips, still puckered. One word.
One syllable.

Just one thought.
  'Why?'

no pause

'I guess I just don't love you anymore.'

blink.

'I haven't, for a few months.'

I-don't-love-you-anymore

—words a hundred percent sure of themselves, certain that
they are headed in the right direction. Like they'd got lost
in the middle taking wrong turn after wrong turn but have
finally found their way home.

He takes back his vows of eternal love, uncrosses all his fingers, and buries his promises as if they were dead and already rotting.

He decides that the gift he'd given me was not fitting *him* anymore, and that it was best he took it back to give to someone else. Someone better? *I love you* remained only a cluster of words. A subset of the alphabet. Sounds, without meaning.

ai lʌv ju

A thing he suddenly could not remember how to mean. *blink.*

My spirit disengages from my body. She glides to our freshly wiped counter, where the spices and herbs sat aligned almost perfectly, and pulls out the fancy-only drawer we said we'd never open.

It's only fair, she says, as she slips out our anniversary steak knife and sticks it into my pounding chest, up and in circles, and up and out. *You need an airway. You need to breathe.*

I turn to the date on the calendar and he turns to the door. The year is almost over though he'd been gone since the springtime. When early April trees were blushing white and pink and the air was getting crowded with nobody but our ghosts.
It was a Thursday.

broken record

i miss y—
i miss y—
i miss y—
i miss y—

i didn't deserve th—
i didn't deserve th—
i didn't deserve th—
i didn't deserve th—

twenty-first birthday

twenty-one years ago tomorrow i was slapped
on the butt and told to start crying. do you see
why i need pain to remind me i'm alive and breathing?

*

my dog died and i couldn't find my heartbeat.
thought we couldn't lose two lives in one day so i decided
if i heaved inside my shirt i could pretend that i was
breathing.

*

my mother calls me selfish every day
and i can't help but start to notice
all my poems are only about me.

*

someone broke into the neighbors' last night
guard said that they stole a couple faucets
didn't understand why they'd steal faucets

but i heard they were so poor they were thieving homes
of taps and metal showerheads—this poem isn't so obvious
anymore, you're thinking about faucets.

*

i have tremors in the shower when i think about running
out of water or being sucked inside the drain hole in a pool
of hair and band-aids. anxiety should be good for my art

like i thought he was good for my body. but anxiety is a
privilege very few are born holding, if you're stealing taps
and faucets chances are you don't suffer from anxiety—

*

you don't have that kind of time. if there's an age that
makes you write about anything but you, i would like
to turn it. to learn how not to fear

those who write about themselves, those who love
their selves and mothers and dogs and hair clogged
shower drains, those who end all their poems

with the obvious.

nine unsettling couplets

From the second my foot slithered out of the blanket
to cool its scarlet sunburns again

I knew I may never find peace; I'll be stuck
counting sheep between dreams again and again

I knew that there were parts of my body
gasping to breathe in full breaths again

that also my nightlamp would not stop blinking
so I pulled the plug out of its socket again

and I knew my fingers still trembled at 90°
conscious to speak in whole words again

so I settled. I tightened the screws on my teeth in
case my lips started to twitch again

for Dave's Double Burger and cream-smothered pants
every Sunday at the altar of Piedmont again

I could hear the thoughts in my head, racing,
struggling to find their pace again

so I got out of bed and drove in my jammies
at 90 on the highway to Wendy's again.

seven degrees celsius

i put aloe vera gel and neutrogena's pimple creams
on the parts of my face that feel less beautiful
than the rest, i palpitate on the 28th of every month
when my vagina takes the reigns over my body

i bleed dumb, turn away, my eyes filled shamelessly
to the brim, let them close before my mum begins to notice
bitter people cry as much as the nice ones do.

i hit pavements and parking lots at seven degrees celsius
in loose black shorts and open-weave sweaters to prove
i'm still quite pretty and frozen and not a lot has changed
this season.

i make my thoughts do cartwheels round *what could have
been*s and *why*s till they hit the ground and fall back into
*let it be*s. i open my eyes and count the flaws around
the stretch of my thighs and wonder why my spine feels
more bent

for the robins that start singing to the chorus
of dawn and walls that blast
morning edm

and when you sit across from me, 1:00 and hot *chai* our
only 2 friends and you mistake my playful sarcasm for hate
i want to tell you i am not half as headstrong and a badass
as i make myself be seen.

it is easiest to pretend in broad daylight than at 3:00
when it's dark and a twisted kind of quiet. i am damaged,
learning from god and VSCO feeds which angles
to curve more at so the sun

finds its way in and it's 5:04 again—restless little blackbirds
pecking at my window pacing back and forth and back
and forth
hitting glass like the heart is for the headless

and i think about why these babies choose to rise before
the sun can even find it's sword to fight the moon it's so
helplessly in love with—

maybe all of this is stupid and maybe i'm the sun you
fucked with and the birds are all our problems.
we're in neptune. this is not our world.
i am not your satellite i will not circle your whims

but god you're funny and you used to say you liked my
bumpy skin
said it gave you ground to plant your big white flag in so
i choose

to let your light burn, for your sake, for the sake of chil-
dren wishing

on your plummet. for their sake i hope you crash and burn
so i can mourn you in the nighttime, so i can put the kettle
on for just one,
so i can talk to all my blisters,
so they can listen.

i am stubborn i play the same playlist on repeat until i'm
sick of it. i will love you till my every bone resents you
because you see every sad song ends the same way
and every sad song ends.

there are very little parts of me i've stowed in secret places;
most of me is in here and you can read me, i am not too
hard a language
though my name never escapes your mouth short of
a slaughtered spelling

i can kiss you with the same lips that light a cigarette
which is to say that i can burn two things with one.
you should watch me
brush my teeth with toothpaste and nicotine,
you should join me, we should
sing sad songs in the winter.

anxiety tastes like

the caress of a cold breeze that slips in around may / and
fogs up / our windows / then wipes them with scotch-
brite / like corn stuck on teeth / there is only so much
thread / to pull at /

like stale chocolate nut crackle / you can tell something's
off / but you still let it linger at the tip of your tongue in
case / you swallow it / and then it's really gone / it's over /
it lives in your belly now / in you /

like empty stomachs / and protineX / and shea butter /
body contouring / hyaluronic acid creams / for dimples
like rebels / stubborn / unashamed / unwelcome / we must
manually synchronize their placement / till our thighs tear
and tremble /

like cardamom / i try to pick it off my plate / i like my rice
plain / to eat in even mouthfuls / flavors add complexity /
and i want to drop some weight /

like rubber / around hip dips / under tongues / on the
fronts of our teeth / on dotted latex inside cheap blue
plastic / in drawers next to pencils and unfinished letters
/ poems / reports due midnight / journals you thought
you'd burn once he left but you didn't / and he did / and
they stare /

when i am twenty

After Aimee Nezhukumatathil

there is a red round cherry atop cream pineapple cake. i grew
up sucking on my fingers, chewing the sides of my skin until i
was too repulsed to be hungry. my mother went from breast-
feeding to careful handfeeding to pointing chiding fingers
at my ribs. what can i say, my skin likes to get away from my
body sometimes. my mother stares with puckered lips at my
tarnished face, pale, stale with *are you trying to kill yourself*s
and *you are going to die*s. she mumbles something critical
under her breath. i smile. she tries. i am twenty and fancy
things up front. cookies, critical claims, questions. water is a
lipophobic substance and i am seventy percent afraid. some
days i think about lunch at breakfast. the girl in my closet
mirror convinced she looks like me. she thinks that my folds
hang like windchimes. i am twenty and with so many birth-
days to fear. will the arbor on my foyer stand taller than me?
could i be my own balloon suspended loose and floating from
ceiling to ceiling, full-faced to faceless—am i helium yet?
am i finally lighter than air? will there be fewer lilies, more
crumbles and pies—apple, chicken pot, lemon meringue. the
air will be shrill, and it will sing of my name. tell me i will
not have to make up the words. swear i will bring no shame.

pull your skirt down

pull your skirt down
add an inch or two to the hem
button up
no collarbones
add an inch or two to the waist
and forget
about dinner
pull your top up
wear a bra
you don't want
to show your nipples
is that a bra?
push the straps in
undergarments
go   under   garments
there are eyes around you
leave
something to their sick imagination
put some pants on
no shorts for lunch or dinner
tell your brother to walk
a little faster in his boxers
sit quiet eat your vegetables—
don't just sit there
go running
get some fresh air
it is never too late
to sweat
but not past seven
there are eyes around you

don't give them something to look at
don't give them
anything
no, he's a good boy
call him
won't you wash your face before that?
put some lipstick on
that's too bold
they like their girls simple
red is fierce
red is power
(red is wrapped in purple and secretly
dumped in the wastebin)
stand tall
sit pretty
be yourself
no just half of that
add an inch or two to your heels
but not too much
let your skirt accent your curves
knees under covers
remember to swaddle yourself
in silk because
you want to look decent
and small.

self-destruct

i am not your damned victim

i am mine

i'm trying to make peace with mortality

i'm trying to make peace with mortality.

i was always afraid of death / yet i've died six times now
/ when she left before i got to say goodbye / when he died
in my mother's arms / when he said he wanted to cut me
into little pieces to feed the stray / when i kept asking for
air and you kept pouring me water / when i came 2 inches
short of home and home picked itself up and moved a
thousand miles away / when i caved /

i'm trying to make peace with time.

i could never learn to be late / always first at all the birth-
days / never fashionable / seven thirty meant seven twenty
nine / punctuality meant precision meant / peace never
came in anticipation of arrival / thought healing would
never delay / she lied / i'd been waiting since may / she
meandered in next march said sorry got held up at cus-
toms, i was not made to feel welcome in your country /

i'm trying to make peace with lasts.

i never cared much for endings / they suck the joy out of
beginnings / they pull the plug on the point of it all / they
leave you with qualms and discomfort / but i love sunsets /
i love colored skies in motion / how blue dies for orange
dies for pink dies for red dies for / black isn't the sexiest
part but it's testimony to change / antecedents of the ever
growing airspace / finales make me cry / so do kisses
on the brow / so do christmas songs / post-its with kind

farewell messages / so do you / and not one of these things is permanent / if i cannot last forever, neither will this grief /

i have yet to write a poem

i have yet to write a poem
that's not about two eyes
and lips that part to speak in
half-truths.

one that's not about my nausea
or the way my stomach coils
inside post-eight o'clock, on
Elliot Road, where butchers
hang dead skins and smoke
their cigarettes.

one that doesn't carry shame
or writhe in pain each time
it bleeds. remember that it
bleeds in lieu of children.

i have yet to write a poem
that speaks of things not loved
yet.

a person, a body, a shade,
a couple different shades
of the sky, of homes not built yet.
that speaks of freshly garnished fish
and soup that takes you back
to *nani's* kitchen when you thought
that life was better without the fish
and soup until you tried it.

i am yet to write
on summers gone and murdered
pests and drinks that fell from
hands that carried sheltered truth
in body bags we wreathed with
christmas holly.

i have yet to write these poems
though a few i like at large still praise
warm umber eyes and tempting lips
and thighs charred with cigarette
butts

and blood brains from wine stains
and pleasure in rain and moments
when rain didn't show:

yes, yes you may
read all of these poems and not fall in love
for my mum says, quite frankly,
we don't have to fall
for all that we touch.

epilogue

i am so tired of writing about love
today,
i will write about me

riptide

you've loved before
you will love again

and one day
you will know what it feels

to surf the same currents
that once sucked you in.

they say it is almost impossible
to ride a riptide

it can kill you—
that last big wave.

they don't know
you are one with the ocean now.

you have kissed her floors
made love in her bed

you have died in her bed

you will swim to the surface again.

april

it got warmer today
the sky came to me in my dreams,
she said she was tired of feeling blue

so I pulled out my canvas and painted her
pink cherry blossoms
like the ones in Tokyo

have you ever felt homesick
for a place you haven't lived in yet
a person you haven't lived for?

my skin does not sear in the skillet
for your kind
I am not your prey anymore

I am learning
there are colors with names
I still do not know

and there is always white space
to fill

My *no* is in my stomach

My *no* is in my stomach
on the outside where it dimples
on the inside it coils
into an oval with no edges
no ends.
It sinks and I wish I could teach it to swim.
It sings when it doesn't like the hand
that touches, lips that pry,
it falls
into a lonesome, yielding slumber.

My *turn* is a full-grown tidal wave
in the center of my gut—
a mirror prejudiced against itself.
My turn is remembering
I can stop.

My *hell yeah* is an underdog.
A lump in my throat that jumps
in good opportunity. It likes to show its face.
It sings along, carries the chorus forward,
It loudens.
It grows in my belly.

She

She trusts too quick and trips on her toes, falls for the
    fraudulent world,
she shuns her own shadow in search of the sun—she looks
    for light in this world.

She cracks open peanut butter jars in one breath, but the
    doors to her heart are half shut
and she tosses their keys into forgotten oceans for the
    brave to discover. This world

is whirling in eddies and tides that have cuffed her—a
    pillar, she heaves her own soul
to the curb when she halts at red lights, for she's seen what
    impatience does to this world.

The bruises on her stomach and whetted knives in her
    throat break silences in rooms dark and masculine,
and the glisten in the corner of her left, wilted eye cries
    justice for one half of this world.

Though still soft in her cries, in her kisses and her lies, she
    throws flames in the truth that she tells,
she can't sing but she can write, for shattered souls, on
    blunted sight—she writes for she *sees* the world.

This earth is far too broken but her feet have battle scars—
she can tell, no longer, of what hurts;
"Apple pies, Neha, I smell apple and—*lavender*. They are
ours to keep in this world."

Someday I'll love Niharika Shah

After Ocean Vuong

     don't be sunless.
there's a little ray that breaks
in from the streetlamp 'round the corner from your window
and you are suddenly under spotlight.
the water that escapes the pipeline down the walls of
broken buildings, forms a puddle:
a grimy goop of all your failings—becomes
your mirror, and inevitably
that's all you see yourself as anymore.

     don't be critical.
you can hear your hips screaming for more room,
smothered beneath skin-tight leather pants
and glitter, as you plunge their heads
into waters that bubble
under satin thongs and corsets
you don't take up as much space as you think you do.
and maybe you do
and maybe that's good,
because what occupies space, we call
matter.
cashews do not grow in the stillness of lakes,
only lilies.

     don't be fearful.
the knuckles you're so conscious about hair sprouting over,
or the skin above your elbows that droops like sunflowers—
they will shed.
and even clouds do

but when peacocks display their array of blue and dance to the
thundering nimbus, men call it beauty.

the fingers you think are shorter and more brown
than you'd like them to be, a carrot stick,
dry in dreary decembers,
will one day be home to a pretty
little
diamond
big
on promises under oath and white bells under church tops.
you'll learn love
is a book you've only read the preface of
and there'll be love-songs and letters about
the rings on your stomach, the way the air drills holes and
stripes
that your thighs are so shy to take pride
over. comfort isn't something that lives in you yet.

        don't be restless.
he is twenty-something, terrified, that he'll pass
before hearing battle-tales your scars have been burning to
tell
since the morning they were first tattooed on.
he is flipping over pages that paint girls
as prisoners, poked and prodded—he cannot see why.
he seeks nature and not numbers so if you think
you can define what makes your body *yours*
in a thousand characters
or less
he is waiting to tell you that if he runs short of words
to describe you

he will make some up.

so he's practicing his arpeggios,
praying quietly to Mary:
*"If today deems me unready,
then someday I will love Niharika Shah."*

someday, you will too.

TO CHANGE.

---

*"I saw that my life was a vast glowing empty
page and I could do anything I wanted."*

— JACK KEROUAC

sonnet for two

what do you do with two lone hearts
that want to do all but repel?
how do you tell broken from broken apart?
which, do you think, first fell?

are tired sighs on the telephone misheard
for a longing, no longer enough?
does your mouth run dry searching for words,
do you call their *i love you*'s bluff?

why do you keep gluing the pieces together
and what do you do with the shards
too tiny to hold, too frayed to measure—
do you hide them in the old brickyard?

does burying the truth in flannel beneath
your tongue allow you to breathe?

love at first sight and other bedtime stories

lies
tattooed
on our skin
   like art

christmas blues

christmas doesn't feel like christmas this year and I don't
know how to stop feeling like christmas can only feel like
christmas   if you come home

december feels like august   half   confused
should it scorch   its people should it rain down
half a torrent   december
doesn't feel like an ending   (like it's ending)

it's difficult   to tell seasons apart   is it christmas
or just another birthday we can't help crying on

like what is there to celebrate   what more is left to mourn

the nip in the air   that smells of peppermint hot
chocolate   and defeat   these hands   look for
another set of hands   afraid of catching fire
          afraid to melt into

my father wants to play silver bells every evening
     and all i want to do is cut my ears out
no silver bells are ringing in the city
our sidewalks aren't busy   and how am i supposed to

want to run towards you and fling my arms around you
          if we're afraid to even touch one another

december just feels like november   on loop   and we
                              can't catch a break

this isn't me asking you to make me a holiday mixtape
        i'm not waiting for you to come home

but if you can somehow make   this christmas feel
more like christmas less   like exile   even from
a distance   then do it   or teach me

teach me to climb the treetop again   hang ornaments we
stole from yard sales back when thrifting was reckoned
child's play   when the both of us were children
    stuffing new stockings   with old stockings

teach me to keep the fire burning without throwing
              all of my past into it

teach me to love photographs for photographs
              curry for   its tang and relish
the world doesn't eat curry for christmas but we called for
indian every thanksgiving and i have to preserve tradition

teach me to love christmas for christmas   for the bitter
    cold weather   for the advent of faith
      for anything and everything   but   you

love and other fertilizers

what kind of love
allows itself to

bloom

and

bloom—
until one day
it decides
   to stop.

alexa, google **love**

> love

pain
/pān/

noun
1. the sign from the universe you keep asking for when you
   can't tell how else to move forward
   "she's obsessed with **pain** because she's privileged
   enough to have it without feeling like it has the power to
   kill her"

Similar: (affliction) (anthrax) (indulgence) (in you)
(a man's sick desire) (his sick body's need)

aubade for erroneous love

can't write about a burning city
            i never fled from home
        just moved.

*

can't write about a mother's kiss
            a father's cry
        on the morning of my very first day   as a poet
everybody says they love me until the forests start a fire
and they find no one else
        to throw into.

*

don't know a better poem   on how to be good
                daughters
                    of this country
its sprawling streets are flaring   with skinny girls afraid
                        to walk
        in heels and *rikshawalas* watching with their
                hands inside their trousers
        i'm too far gone from this city
to save it
i could teach you to extinguish   but when the city burns
            you run blind towards the ocean.

*

i was told only white lies are acceptable   they're like
     marmalade on freshly toasted   skin
i was nineteen and you told me i was *breathing* incorrectly
     i believed you
     i believed my love was waste   if you couldn't even
     teach me how to breathe correctly.

*

forgive me   i
don't understand a family
          that breeds
          on kisses
     i was taught early on to keep my victories   a whisper
that literature only thrives   on the soils of buried litter
and people
          and blood   always proves to be the thicker of
               the liquors
          yet somehow i can pawn it for good price.

*

          i fell in love with metaphors
the day my mum compared me
          to my sister
thought maybe   i could turn

it into poetry
(her)
she is kind but she doesn't understand it's not me
i do not hate her
she's a better daughter   she cooks for other people
she lights candles
i write poems about god and pray he listens.

*

i wish i could sing   about mothers and fathers
and sacrifices born from loving
too much
but the city lamps and ice cream carts
know all our sacred corners
where i go to shed my soft cries
and mum hides her marionette lines
every love i've ever known has left me
burning
this city my mother my father my sister
and you
and you will never be
family.

*

can't write about the city
that burnt
all its people
i have remnants   of the dust

their bodies vowed they would return to

i will take them to the bay for *visarjan*.

they can never return to the city.

you will leave and i will not die

not everything in this life needs to last, to matter.

nothing stays the same

after   all,
ever   breeding
happily   stagnant
            waters
   also
    spill.

this is not a call to love

this is a call to open balconies and cigarettes
and inevitably turning every passing thought
into a poem, and chest pains caused by
nothingness and uneasiness

like mint and diet coke
love is like a science project
(which is to say that i've been failing)

this is a call to trial
to jumping off of trains
of thought
digressing from the point
to write yet another poem

to stumble upon solace all by my
fucking self because i'm all that
i'll ever need and all that crap

to hearts that flip like pancakes
when the phone rings and it's
[insert name] calling because
you're all that you'll ever need—

but what does anyone have against
carving out a second set of ears
to settle your breathing in?

to screens that light up rooms and ringtones
loud that trigger tremors in your gut

until you check and it's not butterflies—it's Dominos
you forgot to unsubscribe

every boy i know is only trying to sell me something
i don't think i even really need:

    extra fries
    cheap cologne
    one more reason to take in one more foster
    (orphaned lovers often think i run a shelter)
    opinions
    burly shoulders
    spare parts for me to fix and send home

this is a call to wake up from the fantasies
our bedtime tales have painted
there are no dwarves no princes
there is certainly no time to sleep

this is calling out to poison that lives and breeds
in diet coke and cigarettes and heavy cream
birthday cakes and the girl who sleeps beside me

so to fairytales and fables and groundless expectations
and endings happy—
happy like nobody even died

and to death that sings of crusades
fought for lovers lost, forsaken,
[unsubscribe]

i have been wearing the ocean

i have been wearing the ocean all day
she has made a home for herself in me
i now take care of the ocean
i drain her weeds and salt her ashes and build sandcastles
of them
i have fallen for the ocean
she lets me cry
there is so much of her
in me
i ask her if she wants to be let out
but the surface of my cheek is the farthest
she swears she'll ever go
i am now one with the ocean
we live inside each other's homes
we wash each other clean of dirty secrets
and sleep to the lulling ghazals of the corals

I smell like a tornado

I smell like a tornado
and this is the part where I spit
out all that's putrid—
every recurring nightmare
that ends with you leaving
with another girl.

I can't tell if it's the lilac in her
hair or the perfume near the collar
of your shirt i always knew was never
yours, or the aftertaste of thunder
in my pants you liked to call
petrichor —
there is nothing here remaining
that doesn't make me sick.

This is the part where I slow down
before the flusher breaks
and I have to eventually stop.

Are you ever able
to stop a tornado from blowing up?
Do you slip in low level air
let it calm the surge
let the clouds take over the updraft
pitting water against dust against
debris is all that is left of you and
me and the residue
from our lungs that burn
with fury.

I can't help but believe that I smell
like a god-sent tornado.

A sacrificial lamb dropped from heaven
with a hatchet and a loose head.

You can tell a lull is coming
when I smell like bread that's molding
and the water in the air starts sticking

You can tell, I smell like a tornado
about to die.

twenty-twenty

to

this year has taken <u>so much</u>

survive

poem in praise of cellulite

After Lucille Clifton

if there is a moon
more hallowed than this
dense as a doormat
brown scruffy and thick   if

there is a moon
more timeless than this
that levitates to the orbits at the far end of jupiter
makes love to a fair europa   if there

is a moon
wiser than this
with age comes wrinkles comes foresight
knows better than to hide behind spanx   if there is

a moon
more common than this
no water into wine just
water   if there is an

end to this moon   if
there is a wolf
in the sky

let it cry as the night changes its guise
let its bones break and morph
into all that is
hallowed and timeless and wise
and common and true

naked

will you love me the same
        when i'm fully clothed

woman (n.) /ˈwʊmən/

object

woman
/ˈwoomən/

noun
noun: **woman**; plural noun: **women**

the one who serves
"the baby she births, the man she beds, the girls she sleeps competing with"

Similar: (lady) (adult) (female) (wife) (person) (but barely)

- ### mother and sister and daughter of the universe
  "a daily woman"

- ### phoenix to all who want to burn her
  "a sun to all who pray"

- ### white winged dove
  "lover of the pure, a white winged dove on the days it rains too loud and heavy"

- ### the other
  "half of human"

- ### the other
  "part excluded from the latter half of human"

Similar: (red bleeding out of her)

- a symptom of passion, a symbol of strength

  "fear woman, love woman, cry woman in your sleep and
  she will shelter"

Leena

a torch of light escapes the sky
with a baby cradled in the gulf of her arm
and the greeks say she is everything
god couldn't be
she is a mother
she is a palm tree folded
in the pages of the quran that men pray to
little girls look up to her hands that wilt to
give shade
their brothers cut branches off her mothered body to
build houses
far away from her
and she trusts that the sky is enough
of a listener and the ocean has tides
high enough to sweep up against the crust
of her sclerified skin
she is wife to a friend
gracious daughter to a hero
she is tender and devoted and the brahmins
didn't name her short of anything
less than brave
she fears god when he's unkind
she soldiers on in spite of it
for the babe that sought sanctum in her belly.

Dear Naina Kapur

for my best friend

Dear Naina Kapur,

How do you write a letter to someone who is literally the
namesake of all of Bollywood?

Naina Kapur.

With a U not double-Os.

U—when will u stop being afraid of telling the world u're
still so pink?

You're only white
on Instagram.

Other places, you're Punjabi.

Why do you hate my version of the world so much? Trash-
talking love doesn't make it any easier to get through.

You worry that I make everything so rosy
like the world's going to wake me up one day and throw
me on a pile of needles.

You worry because you've had to sew me up before
and I'd never looked more empty.

And you'd never felt more helpless.

Naina Kapur.

Stop lying.

To yourself.

Marriage isn't always a contract.
You can want to fall in love with heavy eyes and sandy
skin, and not be cross armed with

*'I'm ENoUgH
fOr mE.'*

It's okay to want to rest against a shoulder that is not
your own.

It's okay to cry

when you laugh and when it's late and no one's listening
to you shuffle your trashy Hindi playlist.

You're an anchor as much as you are glass

-es of tequila.

You're a rebel.

A stinking lawsuit in the face of cheating thickheads.

The sun shines in your belly and sprinkles yellow dust

all over.

There's a reason you go where shadows fail to follow.

You'll get your Happy Ending

at the end.

The sky's the same for everybody
and you're a star —

it's in your name.
You burn regardless of whether people are looking.

The sky's the same, it's screaming
in pink and orange

and you just won't bat an eye.
Stay by the ocean, watch the sun tease her with gen-
tle kisses.

Know that love will find you when it is supposed to

and I already know where you are.
Love,
Neha

fin

the road gets louder
the sky quietens

i'm sorry
our ending isn't quite as beautiful as the others'
but remind me again—which kind is?

there're poems about sunsets, finding beauty
within endings but darling, curtain calls
are only magical and rewarding in the theatre.

it's a tricky thing, the concept of time that
doesn't stop for anything no matter how pretty
and sunsets are proof that it's not the ending we chase

but the part before it—

a quiet evening by the seaboard
the chills of a falling winter
the final calls of a robin distraught on its way home

orange skies infused with a splash of pink and red and
purple
thick at the very bottom, a love so young and raw and
dangerous
fell asleep and forgot it was not supposed to die in the
twilight.

if we loved sunsets for their endings
we would stick around for it.

but the jackets roll down the sleeves again and the rugs roll
back into minivans once the warm orange flame leaves
a big, black, stain
on a canvas that loses all its color.

sunsets make good poems except
we love a sun that's still setting
and silhouettes are nothing but dead.

ACKNOWLEDGEMENTS

When setting out on a long journey you've never embarked on before, you never know how much work it will take to reach your destination. I've discovered along my journey writing *Strawberries Under Skin* that publishing a book takes a village, and I am so grateful for all of the support. Fulfilling this dream would not have been possible without you.

I would not be who I am today without the unconditional love and support of my family. For Papa's constant encouragement, Mumma's soft heart (that I hope to have inherited) and my sister, Niki's unfaltering belief in my ambitions—I am truly grateful. To *Nana*, Jenny *masi*, Deep *mausa*, Vini *masi*, Julius *nana*, Rohit uncle, Sudha aunty, Ruchir, Shreya *di*, Richa *di*, Ryan and baby Vihaan, and everybody in my beautiful, massive, extended family—I am so incredibly thankful to have you in my life. *Nani*, I wish you were here to celebrate my first big win.

To my best friend and support system, Naina. You have been my anchor for more than thirteen years. Thank you for never losing faith in me and for reminding me of all the good things in life we have yet to live for.

To everyone that supported me in the early stages of this journey. Without you *Strawberries Under Skin* would not be a reality. Thank you Professor Eric Koester, Sanskriti Vijay, Priyal Bhojak, Tanvi Tikmany, Anubha Anand, Varun Sampat, Danielle Tarras, Raoul Dubey, Shreya Tibrewala, Shalin Sharma, Rohin Patel, Raj Chag, Ayaan Hussain, Michelle Li, Sahil Agarwal, Naman Jalan, Nishi Patel, Nimish Seraphim, Venesa Gomes, Raghav Gupta, Shreya Sonam Naik, Ritika Gupta, Kathryn Barr, Preet Chokshi, Jwalin Patel, Pankaj Bhagat, Suraj Patel, Ayush Dhall, Ayah Assaadi, Sari P Wisoff, Jahnavi Biyani, Aanvi Kanoria, Shail Saraiya, Jahanvi Desai, Ramya Baddam, Sanjay Garodia, Rachna Sharan, Raju Sharma, Nivedita Singh, Lakshya Dhurka, Priya Parikh, Keerthana Sivaramakrishnan, Krishna Dave, Wendy Aviles, Shrishti Saraf, Gaurav Uppal, Isha Durani, Saad Altaf, Rajshree Jaiman, Akshay Pai, Rahul Kumar, Rakhi Singh, Suman Sharma, Shrishti Sharma, Bisweswar Pattnaik, Manish Desai, Bhanvee Ajay Kumar, Nidhi Bubna, Kapil Dadheech, Kartik Kumar, Prabir Vora, Shayla Herron, Anant Jain, Neha Murthy, Suvigya Seraphim, H Singh, Jeet Oza, Sanjay Dawar, Indranil Roy, Devang Goenka, Sukhdeo Prasad Verma, Animesh Dutta, and Devanshi Banka and family. Thank you Taarini and Anisha for helping design the cover of this book.

Finally, to all those who have been a part of my getting here: Samuel Hawkins II, Ashley Lanuza, Tasslyn Magnusson, Brian Bies, and the entire NDP team. This book would not have come together without your vision, organization, and hard work. I extend my heartfelt gratitude to all of you.